La Llorona on the Longfellow Bridge

poetry y otras movidas
1985-2001

by

Alicia Gaspar de Alba

Arte Público Press
Houston, Texas

para Dolores y Soledad—so full of duende—
and, for the abandoned

This volume is made possible through grants from the City of Houston through The Cultural Arts Council of Houston, Harris County.

Recovering the past, creating the future

Arte Público Press
University of Houston
452 Cullen Performance Hall
Houston, Texas 77204-2004

Cover art "La Llorona Desperately Seeking Coyolxauhqui in Juárez," 2003, by Alma López
Cover design by Adelaida Mendoza

Gaspar de Alba, Alicia, 1958–
    La Llorona on the Longfellow Bridge: poetry y otras movidas / by Alicia Gaspar de Alba
        p.   cm.
    ISBN 1-55885-399-5 (pbk. : alk. paper)
        1. Mexican Americans—Literary collections.   III. Title.
    PS3557.A8449L57 2003
    811'.54—dc21   2003050238
                                                                CIP

∞ The paper used in this publication meets the requirements of the American National Standard for Information Sciences—Permanence of Paper for Printed Library Materials, ANSI Z39.48-1984.

3 4 5 6 7 8 9 0 1 2   10 9 8 7 6 5 4 3 2 1

Contents

Elemental Journey: 7 Days in the Woods (July 1989)

Albuquerque (1990–1992)

Los Angeles (1992–1999)

Land of the Dead (1994–2001)

Tracking La Llorona

I confess: there are those who will tell you that I deride the self-indulgent practice of writers publishing their dreams and journal entries (unless it's a fictional technique, which I liberally employed in my novel on Sor Juana). But I also know that often, some of our best work is tucked away in those stacks of notebooks we writers accumulate like karma. As I have been contemplating how to introduce this second collection of poetry "y otras movidas," I remember snippets of amazingly profound insights I wrote down years ago in one of those notebooks, and I search frantically through twenty years of written karma to find those words, written years before I became an academic, when I had more time than money, when I could afford the luxury to theorize, that is, contemplate, my own poetics. If I knew exactly what I'd said, I wouldn't need to indulge in this archaeology of private knowledge, but all I have is the memory of having said something pertinent. I can feel it there, on the tip of my tongue, the distinct, if subtle, pressure of the words on the loam of my forty-four-year-old brain; but, alas, I must resort to digging, and digging brings up sand and bones and spiders, and an occasional treasure.

Like this, from the introduction I wrote to my M.A. Thesis in Creative Writing at the University of Texas at El Paso (from which I have poached before), titled "Introspection Week: Taking Time Out to Talk about Theoretics, or, Who Says Chicanas Can Write?"

November, 1983

I think poets are crazy in the ultimately best sense of the

v

word. The sense that made us proud in high school when some-
one would say "you're *crazy.*" To be crazy, then, meant to be free
and honest and open to all sorts of things like ditching and *queer
sex.* To be crazy, now, open to the world, is what gives me the
freedom and the honesty to write a poem.

I can always tell when parts of a poem start to synchronize
inside my head, usually in the middle of the night when images
keep rolling around on my tongue and there's no way I can go
to sleep, no way I can close my eyes to that buzzing, shapeless
presence I know is a poem. So I get up and write, not at all cer-
tain what I'm going to say or how the poem is going to look.

The logic of writing poetry, as Wallace Stevens says, is an
"irrational" one; it occurs spontaneously and unaccountably in
the rational mind; it is born of listening to something that can't
be heard except in the deepest crevices of the skull. Perhaps this
is what Manuel Torres, the Andalusian artist, referred to as
"black sounds" when he said "whatever has black sounds has
duende."

Duende, to the people of Andalusia, is more than a hobgob-
lin or a poltergeist. It is a power that expresses itself through all
forms of art. But not all artists, all poets, all bullfighters, have
duende, nor do they all hear "black sounds." These are "earth
forces," according to Federico García Lorca, that exist only in the
blood. They have, he says, nothing to do with aptitude or tech-
nique or virtuosity. ". . . the Duende loves ledges and wounds . . .
he enters only those areas where form dissolves in a passion tran-
scending any of its visible expressions."[1]

I think my duende made her arrival during a crash-course,
six-week poetry seminar in the summer of 1981—my first grad-
uate workshop. I was going through a divorce and living in a
tiny, greasy, roach-ridden restaurant in downtown Juárez. Dur-
ing the day I taught English as a Second Language in the Gen-
eral Motors maquiladoras; nights I was a cocktail waitress at
Monika's, a classy El Paso club. It was at this insane point in my

---

[1]Federico García Lorca, "The Duende: Theory and Divertissement," trans. by Ben
Belitt in *The Poet's Work: 29 Masters of 20th Century Poetry or the Origins and Practice of their
Art,* ed. by Reginald Gibbons (Boston: Houghton Mifflin Co., 1979), 37.

life that I started crawling out of bed in the dark morning hours to write poems. There she was, my duende, pulling on my eyelashes, nudging at my ribs, playing hide-n-seek in my mind. She terrified me. Poetry terrified me because it would take over me, not caring that I had to write on a cold, metal table and squint my eyes under an opaque, fluorescent light.

I wrote six poems for that summer workshop, and at least four of them (in my humble opinion) had duende, that is, they were spawned from the "ledges and wounds" of all of the borders I was crossing at the time. I was leaving my white husband, who was also my best friend from high school and my first poetry mentor, with whom I shared a two-bedroom duplex in El Paso and a purebred basenji named Kenge Bambuti. I was in love with a Mexicana eleven years older than me, who often couldn't afford to pay her rent or her gas bill to that greasy spoon restaurant where we slept in a back room on a broken-down sofa, surrounded by piles of clothing, old shoes, empty tequila bottles. So many contradictions. So many black sounds.

Voice. I never understood what voice meant until I started teaching composition, because that's what was always missing in my students' papers. "Finding a voice," Seamus Heaney says, "means that you can get your own feeling into your own words and that your words have the feel of you about them."[2] I don't know, exactly, what the feel of me is. It has something to do with being Chicana, to be sure, with having duende, with the mental ability to leap between what Robert Bly in *News of the Universe: Poems of Twofold Consciousness* calls "the day intelligence of the human being" and the "night intelligence of nature"[3] and grant consciousness to a stick of ocotillo. The feel of me has something to do with being crazy, with listening to the breath of a poem, with being a chillona, hocicona, butch, rebel of many causes, lover of women and wine. The feel of me has something to do with La Llorona, with being superstitious and overweight, with a hunger for learning. If my words at all reflect these feel-

---

[2]Seamus Heaney, "Feelings into Words," ibid, 265.
[3]Robert Bly, *News of the Universe: Poems of Twofold Consciousness* (San Francisco: Sierra Club Books, 1982).

ings, then I have found my voice.

My voice is also a fronteriza voice. Had I not grown up in an environment so deeply infused with magic and superstition and history. Had I not been able to understand all those horrifying cuentos about La Llorona, that mythical, mystical Wailing Woman of the Mexican and Chicano culture who appears in my writing as everything from ghost to guardian angel, and who is my primary symbol of individuation. Had I never known the feeling of smuggling avocados or cousins without green cards across the border. Had I never played hide-n-seek or held séances in the desert—both great opportunities for noticing the slightest movement of sagebrush, the effect of moonlight on the mesquite. Had I not lived ten minutes away from La Mariscal, the infamous red-light district in Juárez where I spent numerous evenings searching for an Aztec princess named Susana. Had my imagination not been enticed and enriched by this frontera land-scape which bred me, had I been born to only one world, I can't even imagine what kind of writer I'd be, or if I'd be a writer at all. My words, my place on the map—two sides of the same coin.

When I got married at nineteen and changed my name from Gaspar de Alba to Noreen, I instantly lost half of my identity. The only time I signed "Alice Noreen" to the bottom of a poem, I drank myself to sleep. That was the name of an orphan who had stabbed her own mother. I guess I know now why La Llorona has always haunted me.

❧ ❧ ❧

La frontera: a creek, a bridge, a combat zone, a chorizo link between Juárez and El Paso, un sueño—this is my homeland, my point of all departures.

Strange things happen in la frontera. In November 1984, for example, an article appeared in one of the daily Juárez newspapers about an 88-year-old woman named Doña Margarita, who had a petrified fetus in her womb. The anomaly was discovered when the woman, complaining of stomach disorders, was taken to the hospital. X-rays of the patient's midsection revealed a six-month-old fetus, which Doña Margarita said she had conceived in 1927. According to her doctors, the fetus must have died in its 27th or 28th week of gestation and never been expelled by the woman's body. Because it was never exposed to the environment, the fetus became mummified in membranes that enveloped it as well as the womb.[4]

Once, I believed this metaphor of an embalmed fetus to be a good analogy for the place of Chicana literature in the white, wide world of mainstream letters, a literature that had hardened in the womb-walls of "the" community, carried around in the belly of Chicano/a culture but never exposed to the outside world. These days, of course, in the post-multicultural days of mainstream publishing, that analogy is no longer valid. You can find Chicana literature in airports and shopping malls across the country. I see the embalmed fetus differently, now. It's actually not a metaphor at all. It's what all of us—Chicana writers—carry around in our own womb. For me that embalmed fetus is la frontera—crafted of Spanish and English, river and desert, sunlight and mountain, blood and bones and black sounds. This is the landscape of La Llorona, the dream that awakens each time I touch words to paper. French feminist Luce Irigaray, in "And the One Doesn't Stir Without the Other," describes a similar animation:

> A little light enters me. Something inside me begins to stir. Barely. Something new has moved me. As though I'd taken a first step inside myself. As if a breath of air had penetrated a completely petrified being, unsticking its mass. Waking me from a long sleep. From an ancient dream. A dream which must not have been my own, but in which I was captive. Was I a participant, or was I the dream itself—another's dream, a dream about another?[5]

All along, like Dorothy, I've been looking for what I carry inside me.

---

[4]Summary and translation of "En buen estado de salud se halla la octagenaria del feto petrificado," in *Diario de Juárez*, Nov. 1984.

[5]Luce Irigaray, "And the One Doesn't Stir Without the Other," trans. Helene Vivienne Wenzel, *Signs* (1981): 60.

As my friend Susana "Tish" Chávez-Silverman will tell you, this collection has undergone a number of incarnations and name changes. When I realized I had written numerous poems about my father, I called it "Gardenias for El Gran Gurú." When I thought it was a book of poems about death, about crossing the final frontier between life and death, I called it "Chamizal and Other Borders." Now I realize it's really a travelogue, a departure from the Córdoba Bridge that was the organizing principle of my first collection, *Beggar on the Córdoba Bridge*.[6]

Organized according to place, these thirty-five poems chronicle my time in Iowa City, Boston, Albuquerque, and Los Angeles—an archetypal journey north, and then east to west—to end up in the place of all directions, the land of the dead. From the border to each of these places, I have constructed a bridge, and at each bridge, I have seen La Llorona. She goes with me everywhere. To change an old adage a bit: you can take the girl out of the border, but you can't take the border out of the girl. To me, La Llorona *is* the border. She is the voice and the soul and the grief of the border. She is my mother. She is my duende.

The "otras movidas" in this collection refer to short prose pieces that I wrote along the way; they are not exactly autobiography, though they do illuminate certain things about my life at the time each one was written, and they are not fiction, though at times they do employ fictional techniques. They are more like resting places, whitewashed gazebos at midnight where I stopped and thought about how the poetry I was writing at the time, the people who were entering my life, and the places I was inhabiting fused together to provide the lessons I learned on each leg of my pilgrimage. If I'm lucky, each one works as a movement outward that brings me closer to the world around me. In the "Theoretical Introduction" to my Master's the-

---

[6]Based on my 1983 M.A. Thesis, the full collection is published in *Three Times a Woman: Chicana Poetry*, (Tempe, AZ: Bilingual Press, 1989): 1–50. This book, too, had many names, beginning with "Giving Back the World," which was the title of my Thesis. The journal entry quoted in this Introduction has been slightly modified from its original form in the thesis.

sis, I called it "the bilingual, bicultural world that shaped who I am and from whose rich pockets I have taken for years." The poems in the thesis, then, were a gift, a way of "Giving Back the World." When the thesis became the collection *Beggar on the Córdoba Bridge*, the poems told the story of that beggar, me, trading something tangible and material (the coin) for an old woman's wisdom (the world). This world, this "mundo zurdo," as Gloria Anzaldúa named it in *This Bridge Called My Back*, is also the aesthetic and political world to which I pledge my allegiance, which feeds the crazy streak, the poetic madness de una chicana lesbiana fronteriza writer, scholar, and world traveler whose name is Alicia, Alice, Teyali, Tía, M'ija, Honey, La Profe, Gaspar, and Soña Dora.

You don't need a green card or a passport to take this journey. Just an open palm.

Departure
(1985)

Crooked Foot Speaks/Habla Pata Chueca

The first thing I remember—
    the first epiphany,
        knowledge of parts,
            awareness of borders—
was a sudden contraction all around me,
the balloon shifting its course,
a part of me squeezing under bone,
a pain I had never heard.
And the sound of other parts
growing, a constant humming of organs,
music of heartbeat, lung light, thumb, mother.

        Five months later
    the foot stuck
    under the rib
        dragged behind tingling
    in its own little birth
    I remember
        the great mouth
    opening the snap of flesh
    clamps
        on my head
    my crooked foot
    stiff
        with oxygen.

More sounds

Lights flashing

Smell of blood

Blade of cold air

through the ombligo

Hands. Dry blanket

Hunger hunger HUNGER

The memory of parts

This body so different

from that other

that place of original

loss

¡Qué fea!

¡Parece india!

Pelos tan negros.

Pata chueca.

¿Qué le hicieron

a mi muchacita?

¡Pobrecita!

Pero está muy blanca.

De veras, muy blanquita.

Se parece a su papá.

Gracias

a Dios.

Casts on both legs thumping the crib,
white shoes fastened to an iron bar,
crooked roads this side
of the rainbow.

Iowa City
(1985–1986)

In the Shadow of Greater Things

Chernenko's voice croaks on
the six o'clock news.
Lies scratch at his tongue,
flapping their heavy wings
over his speech. I suspect
flocks of black-hatted men
circle the white rooms of his eyes.
How can we hate this old scarecrow?
We call him communist, enemy,
spy, goddamn Red. Blame him
for our own scarlet sins.

                When I left you
my sin was thicker than blood.
                My blame stuck out
its hump and I bore it for good luck.

For two months crow's claws
have combed Chernenko's hair, fed him
his country's last rites.
Wet pads plague his genitals.
His toes hang yellow as teeth.
Already the oven of the earth
begins to burn his soles.
The world is a waiting room
of expectant widows:
Chernenko's death the lullaby
they sing at midnight.

When my father dies
the stories I waited for will blossom.
The lies I told you
will sink in the shadow of greater things.

After 21 Years, A Postcard from My Father

The first time Dad sent me
his love through the mail,
he wrote a letter
and a one-dollar check
for chocolates, he said.
I was six years old, coarse
brown braids, knees like petrified
breasts, granny glasses that darkened
in the sun. I wore shorts under my uniform
and went to Father-Daughter dinners
with my friend Cindy and her dad.
My abuelo picked me up from school.

And Tony (a.k.a. my father)
said in his letter: "Obedece
a tu abuela. No te cortes el pelo.
Aquí te mando dinero para dulces y chocolates."

I changed the one to a nine on the check
and never wrote back. Never cashed
in on Dad's long distance love.

Today, I skip down the stairs
with the knowledge: *my father wrote to me!*
I understand now that this is all
I need to know. I will never see
what has tormented the man
from the day I was born,
the day he called himself a father
for the first time.

This afternoon on the bus,
I watched a retarded boy slapping himself
on the back, a gesture that started
as a caress, his hand moving
over his shoulder as if a cat
or a parrot perched there.

And then the hand grew
wild, angry, tormented, a slapping
that hunched him down on the seat of the bus.

"What's on your back?" I asked him.
He looked at me with eyes that pitied
my lack of vision, my need to know

everything. How could I not see
what his torment was?

"Wings," he said quietly.
"They won't leave me alone," he said.
"They're too heavy," he said.

Dust to Dust

I love dust
along the inner walls of desks,
in the corners of rooms,
on windowsills and cobwebs.
I love dust
on bones, books, TV sets,
on your forehead, mi reina,
your fingers darkened with dust
from the Andes, ashes
of anacondas, jungle dust
the color of twilight
still moist in your clothes,
coffee dust in the suitcase
and the red dust of pottery,
sixteen pieces turned to dust.
Your love crushed, your plans
in ashes all around you, clear dust
of Caribbean salt on my tongue.

The woman who wears my body
squats in a corner
and watches the dust
gather on her lips
like silence,
like shadows of words
that were never spoken.

If you could hear the dust,
if you could learn to love
the subtlety of dust,

the quiet way it grows
over the hearts
of trees and mountains,
over beds and desks and balconies,
if you could trace the journey of dust
through your bones,
you would understand
why I mourn for everything
on Wednesdays, ash days.

Holy Ground

(After the earthquake in Mexico, 1985)

Here in this clapboard house
perched on the pork loins
of the youngest country—
the spoiled brat of the world—
a Mexican, a Colombian, and an Italian
speak of history,
of ancestors shaking up the earth:
the last tremors of faith,
the last hot floes of hope.
Speak of their people suffocating
under all that history
and the three of them
on scholarship in Iowa City,
safe from the oppression of mud,
the crush of buildings and the Vatican.
Safe in this spoiled country
where they too are spoiled
free and rotten as autumn
leaves pasted to this other ground,
this black earth tapestried
in rows of corn.
Yet each one knows she belongs
to her own holy ground,
to a soil blessed by thousands
of bodies left buried where they fell.

The Mexican—progeny of La Malinche—
tries to recreate her doom

in American Studies. Her field
is bar culture, her specialty,
old men with dead wives
and greedy souls: the Scrooge complex.
At George's Bar,
she is the spirit that gives
them back their past, their stiff
heads growing again
in the cemetery light,
beer breath crystallizing
on the stones.

Of the Italian and the Colombian
only their names and loves are known.
What they do in the native
silence of their dreams is a mystery
both of them would like to unveil.

Sometimes nothing matters
more than those envelopes
edged with green and crimson stripes,
air-mailed news they read
over and over in their pastel rooms
in this clapboard house
that was once an abortion clinic.

Boston
(1987–1990)

The Philosophy of Frijoles

In our house we learned how
to clean beans before
the twisted logic of shoelaces.
Before our first confession,
our first nightmare
in the dentist's chair,
our first real orgasm,
we learned the philosophy of frijoles.

Grandma showed us how
to separate the good beans
from the bad beans.
You take out all the dark ones,
she said, *and the old ones*
and the broken ones.
And she'd rake the perfect pintos
into the clay pot, leaving three
little heaps of bad beans on the table.

I always wanted to taste the dark
ones and imagined the wrinkled ones
would boil like the rest.
Never thought the split ones would change
the frijoles' flavor, but Grandma said,
Don't argue. What do you know
about life?

So we took turns cleaning the beans,
baking the rejects in our mud cakes
while Grandma supervised the clay pot.

When we got to Grammar School
we didn't know we were experts
in the philosophy of frijoles,
but only the perfect pintos
could be our friends.

Gardenias for El Gran Gurú

(Day of the Dead, 1987)

I.
Today my grandmother's bedroom blazes
with candles and prayers.
In four years she has added two more names
to the grave list of her dead, one
of them my father's—El Gran Gurú.
His death a *pietá* in her memory.
Her house a shrine
hung with my father's face,
his ghost trapped behind squares
of glass, watching
the beds, the mirrors
la tabla de planchar,
flimsy altar on which she ironed
his starched camisas while he read *Los Miserables*
bare-chested, rum or beer in a tall glass,
dark hair curling up from his ombligo
como un playboy o un daddy del cine.

In the closets,
his suits and shoes move
only when she speaks
the rosary for El Gran Gurú.

II.
Bless me, Gran Gurú,
for I have sinned
in your mother's eyes.

19

I did not go to your funeral:
dust to dust,
indifference to indifference.
I saw you anyway.
Trapped forever in the crystal
casket of your great beauty,
your great wisdom, your manhood
too sacred for children or marriage.
El Gran Gurú too young
to be called Dad or Abuelito.
El Gran Gurú collecting pictures
in a shoebox—old girlfriends,
a son and two daughters
pressed like worms
or promises in your liver.

Gran Gurú,
the only promise you kept
killed you.

III.
At sunset we will take sandwiches,
coffee, copal incense, fresh gardenias
and my grandmother's bright blanket
to the Mount Auburn Cemetery
across the river.

> Papá,
> I have heard La Llorona even in Boston
> in the screech of train tracks,
> in the icy waves
> beneath the Longfellow Bridge.

Other keeners may not be picnicking
among the graves,
rubbing the names
of unknown fathers
with these white blossoms;
but you'll be there, Gran Gurú,
tour guide
to the land of the dead.
This tradition heavy as the earth
over the bones
we two will become.

70 Moons

In her dream the young
    warrior
leaves her nation.
    Sweat
burns down her back.
    Tongue
twisted round a white language, she
    strips
the red bark of her skin.
    Beadless.
Hair chopped to her ears.
    Arrows
turned to chicken bones.

In this world the moon lies
    trapped
in a glass bowl.
    Rivers
run bitter as hemlock sap.
    Hills
stoop under granite.
    Smoke
tangles too thick for signals.
    Mother
this vision is numbered.
    70
moons until we vanish.

Bamba Basílica

In Oaxaca at the basílica
de la Virgen de la Soledad

a radio blares "La Bamba"
in the faith of an Indian woman,

Zapotec, kneeling her way to the altar.
Arms outstretched, she opens

her palms to the Virgin's grace,
una poca de gracia y otra cosita.

Her shoulders rise and fall in the dance
of supplication,

yo no soy marinero, soy capitán.
Beside her, other supplicants

stand before la Soledad
fingers to forehead, mouth, eyelids—

a solar cross suspended
over their disbelief—

arriba y arriba y arriba iré.
Now *la india's* palms come together,

urgent words pressed between them:
por ti seré, por ti seré.

Her head bobs to the rhythm
of a promesa

that Ritchie Valens
never recorded.

Caldo de Pollo

Recipe:
This evening the rain calls
for chicken soup,
thighs boiling their yellow skins
into a broth spiced
with rosemary, basil, and rue—
thoughts of death as thick
as the garlic cloves and the carrots,
more transparent than the onions.

Memory:
A week before my thirtieth birthday
I remember a prediction made by a drunken woman
who fancied herself psychic.

Photograph:
I sit in my one-year-old skin
in the center of a ring of relatives,
my fat fingers hooked
around the neck of a beer bottle.

Three of the six other people in the picture
died in a space of fifteen years:
Grandpa and two uncles.

Prediction:
At thirty, said the drunken woman,
you will join the semi-circle of the dead.

Truth:
The girl died
and became the drunken woman.
The beer bottles and the hard-boiled bones
are in the trash.
The carrots and the grandfather stopped breathing.
The drunken woman climbed the wagon
of dreams and went North.
And the broth boils on,
the chicken blood spiced with rosemary,
the sweet basil of possibility,
the rue and the onions and the garlic
becoming caldo de pollo,
tonic for a rainy night.
29 skins ago, I did not know the recipe.

Confessions

(For the survivors)

1.
Bless me, Father, for my sins
spill out of me
when I think of rape.
(You know what rape is, right?)
When I think of men
with egos softer than pimples,
so scared of lesbians
they rape us in alleys and cellars
stab us on beaches,
use rangefinders to jack off
before shooting holes
through our woman-love.
Tucking that tail
between their own legs
they claim provocation, emasculation,
Sodom and Gomorra as a last resort.
And you sitting here, Father,
listening to my blasphemy
your hard head swollen
with righteousness, meting out penance
like strokes on your dick.
I know what you're up to.
I've been to your trial.

2.
Father, I cross myself
when I think of you
remembering how you slipped
unannounced,
quiet as Gabriel,
into that virgin
place between
my eleven-year-old thighs,
how every night you rested there,
a saint in his hollow,
an angel on the wing
bursting haloes
through my prayers.

3.
My shell is pink and gray
like a clam or a vagina. The whole
place smells like salt.
Further in, it's dark
and moist; when I contract,
Father, how narrow
you make me smile.

You're curious, I know.

A long white beam filters up
the middle of my spine, lining
the back walls like a warm tongue.
You're looking for home,
but not even the pearl
you find is precious.

4.
I eat hearts
of artichoke and palm
I eat wax
that drips from the votive
wicks of prostitutes
and nuns
I eat shadows
I eat thorns
I eat the cinnamon
light of your eyes, taste
of your skin after
you come.

Come, Father, eat
of this body, drink of this
blood, as if the only memory
left in our peckered history
were curled under
the tongue
green seed
sprouting planets.

Pilgrim's Progress

(Tituba, a slave, a piece of Puritan property, was among the first three women accused in the Salem witchcraft trials of the seventeenth century.)

Tituba, the sheaves are out.
Harvest has not known your hands this year.
A noose dangles empty on Gallows Hill.
You're a city girl, now.
In firelight you weave woolen cloth, saved
by a confession you never wrote, black
woman of Barbados, bound to a fortune
not even the Tarot cards could explain
nor the gleaming water nor the dreams
that swept your soul
to the Caribbean hills.

Three hundred years later I walk
under your shadow, another alien
to the white-skinned wilderness.
In shopping malls, train tunnels,
libraries, along the riverbank,
at the museum, in my classroom,
I count the bodies bound
by Progress: the loss of memory,
the quest for a new age.
Salem no longer hangs its witches
except as souvenirs: long-nosed, broomstick-
mounted poppets to hang above the stove.

Tituba, this is what I've learned from living
in this country:
even slavery can be beautiful
if you don't notice it—
the stiff noose of capitalism
cutting your neck—
if you don't start shuffling the cards
or watching the water or
threshing your dreams.

Sor Juana's Litany in the Subjunctive

(Sor Juana Inés de la Cruz, seventeenth-century Mexican nun, scholar, and poet, is hailed the world over as the first feminist and Tenth Muse of the Americas.)

if I could rub myself
along your calf,
feel your knee
break the waters of my shame;

if I could lay my cheek
against the tender sinews
of your thigh,
smell the damp
cotton that Athena
never wore, her blood
tracks steaming in the snow;

if I could forget
the devil and the priest
who guard my eyes
with pitchfork and with host;

if I could taste
the bread, the blood, the salt
between your legs
as I taste mine;

if I could turn myself
into a bee and free
this soul, those bars

webbed across your window
would be vain, that black
cloth, that rosary, that crucifix—
nothing could save you
from my sting.

Listening to Our Bones

". . . the snow falling faintly through the universe and faintly falling, like the descent of their last end, upon all the living and the dead."

—James Joyce, "The Dead"

All season we have been waiting for snow.
The trees whisper *Spring!* but the ground
keeps its hard crust and the ducks
preen icicles from their wings.

This morning the radio announced a storm.
Midday, they promised, eight to ten inches.
We layered ourselves against the arctic wind,
trudged to work, to school, to hay market,
the streets bleached with cold, but no sign
of snow, just the rumors:

It's snowing in Philadelphia.
The storm changes every hour.
One hour till the snow.

> At the King's Chapel Burial Ground
> I watched girls with crayons
> and paper rubbing
> on the graves, the Puritan
> names more eroded
> than the stones.
>
>   Suddenly
> the weight of my shadow
> pulled me down.
> Memory froze.
> The well of language froze.

My life absent as the snow.

I crossed the Common listening
to the gray space in my bones.

By the pavilion, I offered
a hazelnut to a squirrel
and five pigeons
landed on my wrist, one
at a time, like old friends
flapping gossip.

And as I squatted there, stumped,
something scurried up my spine,
a squirrel on my head
crying *Snow!*

The birds raised
their shadows into the trees.
Memory moved again under the ice.
The warm flow of words.
The way home.

The snow descends with the ten o'clock news.
We go to bed trusting in the storm,
not telling anyone
that today we heard the silence
of our bones.
Already the snow is tucking us
into the earth.

Karmic Revolution

I.
Past the China Trade Center,
the Pilgrim triple X movie house,
the Naked Cabaret. Past the caged
chickens at Eastern Live Poultry
and the lucky fish cookies in the window
of the Ho Yuen Bakery,
I look for you, Chinese master
of herbs and needles.

The lump in my throat, the acne,
the cyst in my left ovary, my bad breath,
the biopsy results and the prescription for thyroxin
follow me into the red elevator,
into your office above Beach Street.

You press my neck lightly,
tap my belly, take my pulse
with three fingertips. Whisper each word
of the biopsy report: *no malignancy, focal lesion.*
I want an alternative to killing
my healthy thyroid, I say.
Something can be done, you tell me.
It's a question of harmony, yin & yang,
metabolism not balanced.

You send me around the corner
to the Kwong Ming Company, bookstore/herbstore,
with a prescription written in Chinese.

II.
The man with the long thumbnail says *si'down*.
I watch him lay thin pieces of yellow bark
on a copper balance. *Tang Kuei*, he says.
Stems soft as taffy, *Tang Shen*.
Oblong chips of wooden licorice, *Kan Tsao*.

Black seaweed, ground seashells, dried orange
rinds, a handful of saffron, and a green herb
that looks like my grandmother's *yerba*
para curar empacho.

The *yerbero* wraps your prescription
in white paper and takes out his abacus.
I understand his long thumbnail
as he clicks the thick black beads
of this old world calculator.
Translates into eight dollars and a dime.
No check please.

On my way out of Chinatown
with a six-day supply of your
very strong medicine,
my karmic revolution spinning
dragon lore and curanderismo,
I stop at the Ho Yuen Bakery
and buy two lucky fish cookies.

Galloping

"... In the desert, you can remember your name cause there
ain't no one for it to give you no pain ..."
—America, "Horse With No Name"

I dream of galloping
through the air, thunderhead
of thirty storms pumping
past the blue glass walls
and rehabbed neighborhoods of Boston,
migrating home.

I land in a Juárez colonia,
Mother Night still weaving
her dark sarape over the desert.
An old man shines his shotgun
in my face.

     Squatter, gringa, migra spy, he spits.
I have lived too long
on the East Coast.

     It's me, Abuelo, I say, and move on.

At the crossroads,
three horses race towards me,
hooves pounding dusty spirits
out of the earth. Bare backs
brown and free of trappings,
the yeguas mate;
the stallion joins the gallop
of another race.

I find a truck stop
squatting among tumbleweeds.
The güera waitress in her white apron
tells me I must leave, must go back
where I came from. The horses
are frightened, will hurt me, she says.
                    This desert is treacherous.
She does not know the horses
are my veins, this desert la costilla,
the rib that shaped me.

Mother Night slips her sarape from the loom.
I dream of galloping
into the dry riverbed of my thirty-first year,
thunderbird on the mountain
blessing the valley con lluvia.

Literary Wetback
(1987)

When Bostonians hear me speak Spanish and ask me what country I'm from, I say I come from the border between Tejas and Méjico. Nobody asks me what side of the border I'm talking about, and I don't tell them, mainly because, to me, the border is the border, and it would not make any sense to divide it into sides. It is the place that it is, the country that it is, because of the influence and the inbreeding of the Mexican and North American cultures. As proud and grateful as I am about having grown up in La Frontera, I do recognize its problems, cultural schizophrenia being the one that most concerns me in my writing. By way of explaining what I mean by cultural schizophrenia, I would like to share with you some of the highlights of my formative years.

I was born into a strict, Mexican-Catholic family that treasured, above everything else, all of its ties to *el* Méjico *real:* customs, values, religion, and language. That this strict Mexican-Catholic family had its residence in the United States was a question of economic circumstance rather than personal preference.

At home, I was literally forbidden to speak English, and any of my aunts or uncles could rap me on the head if they heard me disobeying the rule. At school I could only speak Spanish in my Spanish class, otherwise I would be fined a quarter for each transgression. At the same time, we ate Mexican food in the school cafeteria. Most of the women who worked in the kitchen were from across the river, and cheap labor is especially appealing to convent schools.

As you can see, cultural schizophrenia set in early. At home I was *pura* Mejicana. At school I was an American citizen. Neither place validated the idea of the Mexican-American. Actually, I grew up believing that Mexican-Americans, or Pochos, as my family preferred to call them, were stupid. Not only could they not even speak their own language correctly (meaning Spanish), but their dark coloring denounced them as ignorant. Apart from being strict, Mexican, and Catholic, my family was also under the delusion that since our ancestors were made in Madrid, our fair coloring made us better than common Mexicans. If we maintained the purity of la lengua castellana, and didn't associate with prietos or Pochos, our superiority over that low breed of people would always be clear.

To safeguard me lest I become infected by that kind of people, my grandparents enrolled me in a private Catholic girls' school—a luxury which they were certain Pocho families could not afford or even aspire to. To make sure that my Spanish remained "pure," my grandmother had me do two hours of Spanish lessons at home every evening. "Forgetting my Spanish"— meaning not just the language, but the accent as well—was the equivalent of losing my virginity.

But I had no intention of forsaking either my mother tongue or my cherry; both were integral to my survival in the family. English, on the other hand, the forbidden tree of knowledge that I could diagram with my eyes closed, was a reward that my family could never give me, and, therefore, a rebellion. My brother and I used to sneak conversations in English, even swear words, behind my Grandma's back. I would write hour after hour in my journal/portable confessional, playing with the forbidden words and sentences as if they were a hieroglyphics that only I could read. I wrote and performed my first play in the fourth grade, and in the eighth grade I had my first essay published. Neither of those pieces had anything to do with cultural schizophrenia (although the play *was* about racial discrimination), but they had everything to do with my becoming a writer.

I don't know when I decided that I was a Chicana writer, or if I decided at all. It must have happened during my junior year in college, when I was enrolled in a Chicano Literature class, which, of course, I kept a secret from my family. Until I took this class, I had seen myself adamantly as Mexican. Chicanos, in my illuminated opinion, had no language, no country, and certainly no culture. They all wore zoot suits and lived in the tenements of the Second Ward; their graffiti did to buildings what their dialect did to the Spanish language. I was no goddamn Chicana!

How was I to know that zoot suits comprised a culture of their own? That graffiti was symbolic expression, a language of the barrio, as intricate and full of meaning as poetry itself? Who could have told me that Chicanos practiced the same rituals, listened to the same music, believed the same superstitions, ate the same food, even told the same jokes as my purebred Mexican family? Needless to say, my cultural schizophrenia transcended the realm of my unconscious and became a conscious demon, grinning over my shoulder at every turn.

But it wasn't until the Chicano Literature class exposed me to poems and stories about La Llorona, the mythic Weeping Woman of my own childhood fears who more than once had peeked into the windows of my darkest nightmares, that I really started to locate myself within La Raza. Chicanos did have a heritage after all, and I was living it! At home I was Mexican and spoke only Spanish, and yet we celebrated Thanksgiving and the Fourth of July. At school, my language was English and we pledged allegiance to the American flag, and yet we prayed to the Virgen de Guadalupe. Naturally, imperceptibly, this bilingual/bicultural identity became the controlling image of my life, and nowhere did it manifest itself more than in my poetry.

Chicanos are lucky because our heritage straddles two countries and feeds off two traditions, but Chicano culture feeds tradition as well, with change, with individual history, with contemporary vision. In an essay I wrote in the mid 1980s about the place of Chicana literature in the wide, white world, I explained the Chicana writer's role as "historian, journalist, sociologist, teacher, and, activist," like this:

> The Chicana writer, like the curandera (medicine woman) or the bruja (witch) is the keeper of the culture, keeper of the memories, the rituals, the stories, the superstitions, the language, the imagery of her Mexican heritage. She is also the one who changes the culture, the one who breeds a new language and a new lifestyle, new values, new images and rhythms, new dreams and conflicts into that heritage, making of all of this brouhaha and cultural schizophrenia a new legacy for those who have still to squeeze into legitimacy as human beings and American citizens.

So you see, I have always been a Chicana, and I have always wanted to be a poet. The bridge between my identity and my writing has become a symbolic border that I cross at will, without a green card, without la migra or el coyote.

Now there is another bridge to cross, one I have migrated far away from home to find: the invisible bridge between the marginal and the mainstream literary worlds. Like any frontera, this one requires the "right" credentials or the right coyote to get me across. Without either one, all I am is a literary wetback, but that, too, has its own magic.

Elemental Journey
7 Days in the Woods
(July 1989)

1. Adirondack Park

When the map blossomed green
in upstate New York, halfway to Canada,
we followed route 28 north
into this huge green organ,
this wild heart heavy
with lakes and pines,
bear, coon, crow, deer.
Who could have imagined my future
contained such wilderness?

Three years ago, I spread
my grandmother's crocheted blanket
on Revere Beach. She and I wore white
woven Mexican dresses, Navajo beads,
huaraches. We lit candles,
slipped silver bands
on each other's fingers, spoke
our intentions so simply
we never remembered what we said.
To crown the ceremony
she cast white chrysanthemums,
I gave cornflowers,
to the Atlantic, asking the Mother
to bless this joining
of corazón, alma y cuerpo.

Today we awaken to raindrops on the tent,
soaked spruce and wood smoke.
We go for breakfast in town, Inlet
of the forest, amazed at how the hills

swell with mist, float in the distance
like dreams.

Last night, watching the orange print
of the fire, I worried life was too much
of a miracle and she said:

We've learned how to make decisions.
It's deciding that's so difficult,
that makes life seem like an enemy.

Oh Life, oh Mother Planet, you are not the enemy!

From your iron core you speak to us
in your tongue of hurricanes
and droughts. Tornadoes whirl
your message, your great sorrow
quakes under our feet.

In a dream I watched blue
fallout sifting through the earth,
pink particles of a strange light
dropping on the bodies of children,
their mouths oozing mercury
like spoiled fish.

Here in these woods, on this
journey toward waterfalls
I can hear your green heart
and feel blessed, pretend the whole
universe is a child swimming.

2. Swimming in Limekiln Lake

I dived to heal
my lungs, shake
the congestion loose,
uncoil my spine
in the cold water.
Nipples rubbing
on the shallows,
I remembered how
as a girl I played Tarzan
and learned how to hold my breath long enough
to dance with crocodiles,
save Jane
from the water's monsters,
the jungle's ghosts.

I dived to be inside
the Mother's belly,
the end of my thirtieth year
looming like a thunderhead.
Once I was afraid to die
at thirty. I know now
each birthday is a death.

The reeds growing in the lake
slough off my used skin, the past
rises from the water like steam.

3. Waking Up in Ontario: Reward

Because we were lost, because
we had not reached the Canadian woods

and had to pitch camp on the lawn
of Knight's Hideaway Park,

we turned our tent
to face the trees, our back

window to the row of trailers
rooted in the electric lots.

Our lot dark as the Adirondacks
though we heard no branches

breaking three feet from the tent,
no black bears,

no deer or raccoon sniffing
at our Birkenstocks.

We slept like tired girls,
hardly moving, our dreams

weighing down the night.
The darkness, the moist grass, the stars

swarming silver through the oaks
marked the trail to the Mother's womb.

Nothing in our dreams predicted
that sunrise convergence of song,

how the trees blazed with warbler,
robin, blue jay, redwing blackbird,

sparrow, crow—their voices bursting
like fireworks out of the leaves.

4. The Niagara River Speaks Three Languages

Upriver
Up here, there's no hurry.
Willows tilt along the bank
and creeks spill like childhood
memories into the flow: the time
Grandpa bought me a dwarf-sized shovel
to help him plant rosebushes in the backyard;
the time I rode a bus to Disneyland,
nine-years-old, no family, the tour-
guide my father's girlfriend; the time
I came home from school and found
our dog Sansón stiff under an army blanket.

The paved road by the water
is hardly used. All the attention
is nine miles downriver
where the Falls fill cameras
and absorb the energy of every tourist.
If you don't believe me,
notice, the next time you ride
the Maid of the Mist, how your heart
rattles as you cross the rainbow, almost
at the foot of the Falls, how your lungs
heave and nearly break open in the wild
splashing and churning of the water.
Notice how exhausted you are
after humbling yourself
to that part of the river.

Up here, there are no expectations.
Every creek and bridge you pass,
every picnic table and docked boat,
every tent and window breathes
of solitude. You can build
up your strength on this quiet
Canadian road.

The Falls
You see, even if I am boycotted
by the grandmother who pressed warm
flannel cloths to my chest when cough
stormed my lungs, and even if
the uncles who took me to the movies
and gave me quarters for domingo turn
their shoulderblades to my lesbian
life, I will keep thundering
through the course I have chosen
to carve for myself. True,
the falling, roaring tumult of water
separates two countries.
This border is wider and more dangerous
than the Rio Grande, but the bridge
balanced over the gorge is called
Rainbow Bridge. The iris
is another infinite lesson.

Whirlpool Rapids

It used to be popular to tempt
the rapids. Men and women in barrels,
on tightropes, hoping their names
would be forever linked to Niagara.
Such a whirl of human folly,
this thirst for fame, this need to compete
with the Mother's power. Today,
in a small room two-hundred-thirty-feet
into the gorge, the daredevils' names
and pictures decorate the walls.
You forget them as soon as the rapids
crash into view, or you shake
your head at their courage, their choice
of a shortcut to the Otherworld.
Of course, not all of them died.
Some were found tumbling in the whirlpool,
deaf and dizzy, but more defiant
than the water breaking on the rocks.

Through the canyon of my life,
defiance is a vein of flowing crystal,
fed by rain and tempered
on ninety-degree turns.

5. Rainstorm: The Gorge

The suddenness,
like everything else,
is a gift,
a way the Mother has
of inviting you to listen
longer, learn the three
languages of the river.

At Boyer's Creek the river spoke
a whispered, ancient tongue
that lapped at the stones
of your memory.

At Horseshoe Falls you trembled,
the wild mares of the moon
galloping into your bones.

Here, the rapids roil with lust,
churning like the wet
dream of a giant woman
in whose depths the gorge
is but a ligament
to an even deeper
and more electrifying
storm.

6. Piseco Lake

Back at Adirondack Park
I watch a blond boy
smoothing a space on the beach
for the sandcastle
that will moat his loneliness.
Other boys shout *Marco!*
Polo! in the water
and three girls chase
after attention in their tight suits.
The castle builder dips
his pail into the lake,
mixes the water with sand
to shape his walls and towers.
I wonder if he remembers
the Mother's song or the cave
walls he painted with buffalo blood
in another life.
I wonder if he will grow
into a man who cleaves
to another man,
to poetry or photography,
if he will choose
not to attend his father's funeral,
if he will take an elemental journey
like this one
and find himself
on the edge of water
inhaling time
as quiet
and luminous
as the heart of quartz.

7. Point Comfort: Coming Home

Humpbacks in the clouds
hedge this amethyst twilight.
The lake surrenders
its clarity, swallows
the misty secrets of the trees.
Potatoes roast on the fire
as I slice onions, watching you
shoulder camera and tripod
to Lake Piseco's shore—
the negatives
of all the water
you have shot swirling
in the dark room
of your memory.
The light you cannot dodge
or burn will blaze from the bones
of these images.

It would be so easy to return
to the earth without a purpose
or a coffin. Life is enough
to humble anyone.

The evening grows its black fur.
I toss greens, transfixed
by this love affair
with the woods,
this birth of silence
over the water.

You and I will leave
the North heavy
with joy,
black bears fishing
in our blood.

Albuquerque
(1990–1992)

Autumn Equinox in the Sandias, 1990

I. Ritual
Sunday morning and the mist moves over the mountains
like blue water, a spirit lake rising between the pines.
The rain comes quietly, drops thick and slow
as the sap bleeding from this wounded ponderosa,
a sharp green smell oozing out of the bone-
colored wood.

We are three daughters seeking a ritual of balance.

II. Grief
On flat rocks, she builds an altar, smoke of
copal and pine resin rising from the iron bowl,
blessing the skeins of llama wool she brought back
from Argentina last winter. Every night her gaucha
hands weave the dark strands of a mother's
silence, the white cords of an hija's grief.

III. Ghosts
She burns two leaves, reads a white-winged chant over the incense.
At the foot of the ponderosa she carves a grave,
folds the ghost of the little girl, niña de La Llorona
left on a riverbank years ago, into the earth.
The sap will sweeten the dark ground,
the mound mulched with pine needles, marked
by a lavender aster.

IV. Shame
Wrapped in damp green, a soft shell, I sip vodka
in the rain, witness, chronicler, offering these black
flakes, these charred words picked from the bone
heap of father memories in my throat. "Your Papá
can't stop drinking because of you. *¡Qué vergüenza!*
¡Qué castigo!" A daughter who loves women.

V. Prayer
Silent mother, vacant father, deserted daughter—
in this ritual you form a trinity of thorns.

We knit, chant, burn bitter incense to salve the wounds.
We funnel the mist, inhale the breath of piñones with our embrace.

While we share poppyseed cake and coffee in the car,
our steady voices steaming the windows, another
daughter is uncurling out of her cave, my sister's womb.
Equinox: buried ghosts, breathing child.

VI. Balance
The quest for balance is a long climb inward.
Morning hikes into the ether mountains of memory.
Unmarked trails ten thousand feet above the valley.
The knees sore. The ankles uncertain. Sticky sangre
de ponderosa to anoint the throat and eyelids.
Pine cones to ease the fists open, like forgiveness.

Bluebirds

1.
It was a Thursday
evening in Santa Fe, blue
with snow and we were so
new at this old dance.
You poured me white wine and said,
"What else can I give you?"

Transfixed in the kitchen
by your smell, your black chemise
under the loose buttons of your dress,
I tracked you to the well where women
sink clay jugs into water and sing
their swollen hearts to sleep.

2.
And Gretel said, "let me return
to this doorstep," leaving her trail
of bluebirds, bread crumbs,
and falling stars.

3.
On hands and knees we climbed through snow,
our first ritual. I buried nuts
from my altar like afterbirth
to feed earth and squirrels in Spring.
You made a circle with corn-
meal and beans, pine needles,
and red chile seed—sand painting on snow,
copal burning in the center.

I remember how you held on to me,
your black hair on my shoulder,
our breath rising like copal smoke
into the arms of ponderosas.

Later you scattered sweet
yellow bread
for bluebirds hiding
in cedar and piñón. They soared
to the bare ribs of scrub oak,
filled their iridescent beaks
with your offering.

4.
On the road from Santa Fe,
the sky slipped into her palest
green rebozo, fringed in gray cloud,
and called it twilight.

You asked if I would ever leave you
and the bluebirds
caught in my throat
broke like promises
into song.

Chamizal

(Historical note: In 1963–64, the hundred-year-old border dispute between Mexico and the United States was settled by virtue of the Chamizal Treaty. To stabilize the course of the Rio Grande, the Chamizal Convention isolated 796.5 acres of land along the Juárez/El Paso border, 193.2 of which were transferred to the United States, and 603.3 to Mexico. It is the only piece of el Norte, lost to the United States in 1848, ever returned to México.)

(for Deena)

Tonight Sangre de Toro
slips smooth and cool
as prophecy
down my throat
or your tongue
tasting the deepest parts
of my hidden name

In your mouth I am
Teyali

Daughter clinging to a chain-link fence
watching the bad woman whose name
shamed me, Mamá
driving off in a strange man's car

At Christmas and birthdays
she gave me Barbies
that I impregnated with cotton wads
and left in a drawer

to wait for the moment that never came
never too thrilled about playing with dolls
until now
contigo, muñeca,
mujer who loves the one
I've hidden

In your mouth I am
Teyali

Handsome woman of your dreams, me dices,
whose hands draw out of you
your own secret self
the absolute gentleness
of your gaze bathed
like your house in blue light

A November afternoon
sitting across from you at dinner
plates of arroz con pollo
the pungent oregano
of our desire
poetry haunting my tongue

In your mouth I am
Teyali

Four years old
and two women talking custody
my mother and my father's mother
going to court

I dream a chain-link fence
between Teyali and the ocean
in the distance the Guadalupe mountains
curve out of the earth
like solid breasts

I shovel the sand under the fence
but cannot tunnel back
to that body
of water whose name
was carved out of my tongue
the same name as mine

There are two of me and I
have always lived between two women
bridge, river, desert
claimed like el Chamizal
first by one country
then the other
broken treaties in my wake

In your mouth I am
Teyali

Blindfolded woman
holding two swords
across my heart

The tarot positions you
in the place of fate
High Priestess
you open me so gently
fold the pages back
and my history rises
like braille
under your fingers

Me preguntas, where have I been?
how did you find me?
I am the one with the shovel
the one digging for restitution

In you, in the deep gate of your body,
in the wet welcome of your mouth
I meet Teyali.

Name that Border
(1991)

1959

What name are you giving her?

Teyali.

That is not a Christian name.

It is her mother's name.

If you want her baptized in the Church, you will have to give
her a Christian name.

Teyali Alicia.

Alicia.

Alice.

1979

Teyali. My name has always been a trauma to me. My real,
first name, that is. My secret. Marking up my birth certificate
like a deformed footprint. This is an overreaction, you might
say, and indeed it is. Why shouldn't it be? I was brought up by
paternal grandparents who used that name to mop up the floor.
You see, when I was five, my parents were divorced and the
blame was, naturally, placed on my mother, accused of being a
bad wife and a bad mother, Teyali Senior. I remember cringing
as a kid whenever a neighbor or a cousin forgot and called me
the bad word, the bad name . . . Teyali.

1983

Alice. The Christmas before eighth-grade graduation, my
best friend, Betty, gave me a lavender book of bound, ruled
white pages. This became my very first journal, a portable sub-
stitute for the confessional that I had relied on to cleanse my
soul, at least until sixth grade, when the priest told my grand-

mother my sins. Here in this lavender book I would tell all my secrets, exorcise all my sins, and not have to worry about penitence or forgiveness.

The first thing I wrote in that diary was my name, eight different colors, a rainbow of me's: blue, black, red, pink, orange, purple, brown, green. *Alice Gaspar de Alba* on every line of the first page, as if the colorful repetition could blur the fact that *Alice* wasn't really my name. She was the character I wanted to be, the girl who spoke English like a gringa, the girl whose first name was always pronounced right, the girl whose Mom attended Girl Scout meetings and whose Dad took her to Father-Daughter dinners at school. *Alice* was my looking-glass identity, one that showed itself, at first, only in the wondrously silent pages of that lavender book, and that has stayed with me for over half of my life.

1984

In this dream I am at the beach with my grandparents. Pa' Carlos sits in a lawnchair in his bermuda shorts, reading the newspaper in Spanish, *El Fronterizo*. My grandmother, in a black one-piece suit, her hair tied back in a yellow scarf, is spreading our lunch on a sarape stretched over the sand.

There are three of me in this dream: two Alices, aged twenty-six and nine, and one Teyali, age four. The twenty-six-year-old is my present self, the spinner of the dream, who wanders into the scene. The four-year-old, Teyalita, is stubborn and energetic. And the nine-year-old in long braids (who is Alice at school but Alicia at home) is transfixed by the sea. Both of the younger me's are standing at this huge chain-link fence that separates us from the ocean. There's no way of getting to the water because of this fence. The four-year-old has her little shovel in her hands and she's digging furiously in the sand. She wants to make a hole under the fence to get to the other side. She doesn't

70

want to stay where she is. The nine-year-old just stands there, her fingers hooked on the links of the fence, feeling the breeze, staring dreamily into the sea. There is a yearning in her eyes, but her face looks resigned. In the background, my grandmother calls out: *"Alicia, ven a comer,"* come and eat. And then I hear her saying to me, the dreamer, *"you were always so hungry."*

1985

Right now I am weeping about loss, about its inevitability, the irreducible reality that is loss, that always, no matter how trivial, each loss changes us in some way. Perhaps loss is what we mean when we say "growing up." Perhaps loss is the process of maturity, the way a snake matures by losing/shedding its skin. A name is a skin.

Yesterday, I shed *Alice.* I was sitting on a rock wall, some-where in Mesa Hills, between the thunderbird and Cristo Rey, watching a red sun setting in a green twilight behind the Guadalupe mountains in Juárez. At my back, one of those dark summer rainstorms that rise suddenly over the desert was approaching from the east. And it seemed to me as I watched the sunset that it was *Alice* who was going down in that blood-tinged wash of light behind las colonias. And I realized that, despite the scars and the loneliness that characterized *Alice,* hers had been a fiery life, relentless in its heat, and it was ending in the same place where I had shed the most skins, forged the most poems, the border. *Alice* taught me all that I know about lan-guage and love and heartbreak. And when I turned my back on her, on the last rays of the sunset, the dark clouds I was walking into, the rainstorm fisting over the thunderbird on Mount Franklin, the cold gray tunnel of the street—all of it spoke to me of birth, the birth of my new skin whose name is both old and new to me, in English or Spanish: *Alicia.* I didn't even contem-

71

plate at the time the contradiction of my English-named self set-ting south of the border while my Spanish-named self was being born in el norte.

I am leaving the border after 27 years. Right now, on the plane to Iowa, where I'm going to begin a Ph.D. in American Studies, I understand that from now on my life is hinged on flight. My past self, my make-believe looking-glass identity, closed its orange eye under the Juárez mountains. My present self is emerging out of these heavy grey clouds that surround the plane, roller coasting in the sky, wings dipping, pushing through thunder. The clear presence of storms.

1990

My lover and I have come to spend Christmas with my mother and family. Tonight was our first evening here, and we had an intense opening-up session, talking memories of my childhood and of my mother's life with my father (so strange to hear them talking about a time I have absolutely erased from my memory, to think that I spent any time at all with my mother's side of the family before the divorce). We spent all afternoon and evening helping my Abuelita make bizcochos and buñuelos for Christmas dinner, and the stories were spilling out of my grandmother as though she'd been collecting them just for this moment, a rich anthology that I counted as my gift from an abuelita I hardly know.

She remembers how I used to cry as a child when my par-ents left me at my grandparents' house (this must have been before my mother decided to leave my father), and how I used to cling to the fence and cry out: "*¡No me dejes, Mamá, no me dejes!*" Don't leave me! A cry, Abuelita says, that used to echo in the streets of that Clardy Fox barrio. I think of La Llorona, the Weeping Woman, whose wail haunts the riverbanks, the arroyos, and the ditches of all the barrios of my people. The mother crying out for the lost child, only in this story, it's the child crying out for her lost mother. But it's that one detail that snags me.

What fence, Abuelita? I ask. What fence was I clinging to? The hinges on this tiny window in my chest begin to squeak. Something is moving around in there, pushing to get out.

The chain-link fence around your grandparents' house, she says.

Suddenly I know what that old dream means. The chain-link fence at the beach. My grandparents and the different incarnations of myself on one side of the fence. The inaccessible ocean on the other side. The missing link, the suppressed memory emerges out of that tightly shuttered space. The ocean is my mother and I can't reach her. Ocean, archetypal mother, my four-year-old self couldn't dig her way back to you. I resigned myself like the nine-year-old in the dream to living on this side of the fence, in my grandparents' garden.

But the fence marks not just the boundary to my grandparents' property. It's also the Tortilla Curtain, and the barbed-wire gate between the four-year-old who hasn't been brainwashed yet into hating her name, her mother's name, herself, her mother; the nine-year-old who kept her Barbie dolls as secret as her name, who dreamed of a family as distant as the ocean, who crossed through the looking glass into a motherless land; and *Alice*, the Chicana lesbian poet who, like a Monarch butterfly, migrated south to prepare for that archetypal journey north, away from the border, the desert, Aztlán, the mother, the lover, the secret self. Alice/Teyali/Alicia. The border that runs down the middle of my back is my own name.

1991

I have two brothers and two sisters; three of them call me Alice when speaking to me in English, Alicia when speaking Spanish. One calls me Teyali, a name she loves so much she gave it to her own daughter.

¿Cómo te llamas? I ask my niece.

Teyali, she says. I am Teyali.

There is nothing ugly or painful in that name for her, and it hurts me, it hurts my mother, to think that I was my niece's age when they took away the beauty of my name and left the ugly secret, the deformed footprint, in its place.

Alice was with me for twenty-seven years. Now, I am Alicia. Chicana from the border who can speak Spanish like a Mexican and English "without an accent." Lesbian/tortillera who shames her family because she loves women. Radical feminist who isn't politically correct enough to find the rhetoric of separatism convincing. Mujer de color whose skin and phenotype have often been "praised" for not looking Mexican. A Ph.D. candidate. A child archaeologist digging a path to her own lost land.

Teyali is a border I cannot cross.

Los Angeles
(1992–1999)

The Waters of Grief: Día de los Muertos, Santa Barbara, 1992

(para las Bloomies)

1. *Setting Sail*
We are riding the waters of grief.
In our three ships
we drift toward discovery,
our silence at full mast,
charting a course
by the astrolabe of the heart,
the flat mirror of the open sea
holding us up, like a nightmare,
or the faith
of a round world.

2. *La Niña*
"¿Qué dice? ¿Qué dice el doctor?"
the mother's voice rasps
in the child's ear. She is responsible
for Mamá's life, but her seven-year-old
vocabulary is not fully forked
in the two tongues.

What cannot be translated
floats away, hardens, a chain of islands
caught in the throat,
misnamed in the hazy latitudes of memory.

3. *La Pinta*
The blond boy squints at them:
old Dineh woman dressed for town,

blue velour and silver belt,
great granddaughter at her side,

Chicanita of three summers—
crooked braids, freckles on brown skin.

The boy knows his place on the map.
"Squaw!" he states. His white tongue

lacerates the old one's face, legacy
of scar tissue weighing down

the child, the name anchored
in the blood of a nation's history.

4. *La Santa María*
The cats feast on our Old World
rodents, howl like the gale
of a high noon northerly when we
cast their litters to the sea.

*"Hasta una gata es mejor madre
que la tuya,"* she says, pumping
the iron pedal of her sewing machine.
"Una gata nunca se separa de sus hijos."

You learn about the motherhood of cats
at age five; your mother's absence a compass
through the journey of your life,
a wound you steer by,
as private and precise as the pain
of mutilation. Thirty years later
you are still seeking different routes
to that motherland, only
to shipwreck again and again
on the same old rocks,
the beaches of every paradise you find
littered with drowned cats.

5. *Discovery*
We are writing the waters of grief,
the tides of language that
tossed us out of the country
of our innocence.

In these uncharted lands we discover
the ghosts are not generous,
will not trade
their gold for our beads,
their stories for our glassy silence.

Like midwives of memory we sever
the knots under the tongue,
sing our eulogies
to the wind.

Huitlacoche Crepes

(for Antonia and Arturo)

I.
Your friend tells you she is afraid
she has lost her voice
somewhere in the surcos
of her hot Texas memories.

II.
At the reception a woman shakes
your hand, tells you how magical
your story was and how Mexican
literature is so loved in this town
she calls "plain vanilla."
You wonder if she has ever tasted
the chocolate chips and mocha swirls
the strawberry juice marbled
like blood in the jasmine-scented earth
of San Antonio de Bexar.

III.
The güera journalist sits
at your table—thick plates of cabrito
and huitlacoche crepes, café de olla—
and asks the Mexicans who got there
first what they think about bilingual
education, and doesn't immersion
make much more sense if the goal
is to become American citizens?

IV.
México always reminds us
she is there—in the pall of smoke
that stretches over the border,
on the brown backs of travelers
bent low over beets or strawberries,
Virgin of Guadalupe tattooed to their
shoulder blades or dangling from the rear-
view mirror of their American dreams.

V.
"What do you think about bilingual education?"
The question hangs in the air, obscene
as the flash of exposed genitals. A sarape
of silence falls over our chocolate-
dipped strawberries.
Do the Mexicans get up and leave?
Beam us up, Scottie!
Do we throw the gourmet fungus
huitlacoche crepes
in her face, lecture her
about beans and corn and strawberries?
Do we take a sharp blade
to her native lengua,
slice all the way down
to the agave heart of silence
where nothing but mezcal grows
and the tongue shrivels like the worm
at the bottom of a bottle labeled
Freedom of Speech?

In another year, every immigrant's
new social security number will be
187-209-227.

VI.
Write about your feet, you tell your friend,
about the earth your toes have traveled,
the surcos
where you planted the seeds
of your working heart, where your mother
and father pulled the master's tongue
out by the roots, immersed it in
the hundred-and-twelve degree glare
of the south Texas sun while their Mexican
voices filled the fields with song.

Neighbors

"How do you debark a dog? Cut out its larynx?"
"That's how some people do it. But he has such a thick
coat, I don't want him cut. They'll just go in through the
mouth and slice. That way my neighbor won't be calling
me all the time to tell me to shut up my dog."
                    —Anonymous hallway conversation

They'll just go in through the mouth
and slice, she says, solve this
neighborly squabble with a simple
mutilation, the dog's thick coat
intact, his bark an echo
in the bruised tunnel of his larynx,
his wound buried deep in the throat.

Nameless dog, your language
offends the neighbor.
He finds your lack of interest in his sleep patterns
"unacceptable," files a complaint with the county,
circulates a petition, registers
those who haven't voted.
Righteously, they sign their names.
Yes, remove that hateful sound,
that dirty dog language
keeping us awake at night. We are afraid
of not understanding what those dogs say.
Amputate the vocal chords,
sever the memory of the canine tongue,
keep them caged and quiet,
obedient as muzzles and choke collars on a leash,
that we may sleep more soundly

not worrying, not wondering
when the dogs will come
and take our jobs, our homes, our health
care, we the law-abiding citizens
who own the dogs.

Years ago a basenji shared my life,
breed so primitive it couldn't bark,
voice box made for yodeling
to pharaohs and pygmies.

Descarada/No Shame: A[bridged] Politics of Location
(1994)

My work is about resistance, about the legacy of resistance that flows through my veins as a Chicana lesbian/butch/tortillera feminist from the border. In that list of appositions that define me, which came first? I became a Chicana at twenty. I became aware of myself as a fronteriza at twenty-two. Although I wasn't formally a feminist until I reached high school and fought for the rights of female athletes in my editorials, I had always gotten in trouble for being the wrong kind of girl: the kind that talked back, disobeyed, and wasted time. As far as my lesbianism—well, I think I always loved girls, even when I didn't want to be one, even when I thought butch was better than femme any day, never mind that femmes gave me the kind of dreams that tortillas are made of.

Back talk and disobedience were outward manifestations of my resistance to both my family's and the school's patriarchal domination, dogmatically enforced by my grandmother at home and the nuns at school. Wasting time, or rather, reading stories and writing in my journal rather than cleaning the house and memorizing the Act of Contrition, was my inward resistance. In my journal, I used English, a language foreign to my family, and the medium through which I talked back most forcefully. I used English to curse at the injustices of my young female life and to construct fictions in which the protagonists defied the social codes by engaging in, for example, interracial relationships, masturbation, and Mother Superior matricide. In my reading, I solved crimes with Nancy Drew, stirred cauldrons with Morgan le Faye, jousted with Sir Lancelot, saved Jane from alligators and snakes, joined Dracula in his nightly forays for fresh blood.

I married for the first time at six years old; the neighbor girl who was my wife wasn't allowed to walk on her own; in other words, I didn't let her walk; I wanted to carry her everywhere. In my innocent domination of her, I was acting out what I saw— my uncles' and grandfather's oppression of their wives. Her lack of agency was precisely what I, growing up as a girl, unconsciously resisted.

At twelve (probably as a result of the witchcraft kit I had hidden in my closet through which I learned to channel the wisdom of powerful women), proving Simone de Beauvoir's theory that "one is not *born* a woman,"[1] and foreseeing Monique Wittig's notion that "lesbians aren't women,"[2] I chased after my friend Giselle, frightened her constantly with my insistence that she look under my uniform to see that I really wasn't a girl.

At sixteen, I opened my legs to my boyfriend and kissed a woman, both for the first time. In my journal of that period, I called the former, which I now realize was date rape, "the most beautiful and fulfilling experience of my life, the immortal sacrifice." I called the other event a trap, a nightmare, a morbid web of lesbian love in which I had been inadvertently caught (notice the passive voice). The truth is, the immortal sacrifice bled like hell, and I couldn't walk without pain, or piss without it burning, or play basketball for nearly a week. The morbid web of lesbian love had been spinning in *my* innocent mind for years.

The truth is, *she* excited me. Her gentleness, her aroma, the way she blushed whenever I stared too hard. I liked sitting next to her in her car, listening to our favorite song, "It's Magic." I liked teaching her to swim in the pool of the Ridgemar Apartments, at sunset, when there was hardly anyone around to see me stroke the wet skin of her arm. And, the night of our first

---

[1]See Simone de Beauvoir, *The Second Sex* (New York: Alfred Knopf, 1952).
[2]See Monique Wittig, "One is Not Born a Woman," *Feminist Issues* 2 (Winter 1981): 47–54.

kiss, on our way to the Circle K to buy ice and cigarettes for the party going on at my house, she confessed that she loved me, that she had never felt that way before, that she was afraid. I held her in my sixteen-year-old arms and felt carnations exploding in my chest. I remember how the car zigzagged down the dark street, an orange Love Bug climbing onto curbs, floating past stores and houses. No memory of ice or cigarettes or time. Just that warm, wild drifting into the night.

Three months after my wedding to the white man who performed the immortal sacrifice on me in the back seat of his father's car, I started a story set in a gay bar. I had never been to a gay bar, and wrote such an outrageously ridiculous description of the place, that my husband suggested I go to a real gay bar with one of the "girls" he worked with who was bisexual. (For that, I shall always be indebted to him.) She and I went to the Old Plantation in El Paso and ended up staying, dancing, talking, until last call. Afterwards, we went to her apartment, and I spent the night. I remember after making love to her opening my eyes and seeing that it was dawn: both a literal and a symbolic awakening. From then on, I knew consciously that I loved women, and wanted, more than anything, to make my life with a woman. Not that it was easy to leave my husband, to come out to my family (my grandmother didn't speak to me for two years), to label myself a lesbian. Despite what I knew about myself and what I desired, homophobia was still informing my existence. As Gloria Anzaldúa says, homophobia in many ways is "the fear of going home. And of not being taken in. We're afraid of being abandoned by the mother, the culture, la Raza. . . ."[3]

Of course, I had not read *Borderlands/La Frontera* (it wasn't in

---

[3]See Gloria Anzaldúa, *Borderlands/La Frontera: The New Mestiza.* (San Francisco: spinsters/aunt lute, 1987): 20.

print, yet), and I had never heard of Gloria Anzaldúa or Cherríe Moraga. If I want to really shock you, I should tell you that in 1978, as a sophomore in college, I didn't even know the Chicano civil rights movement had come to El Paso, although I had been introduced in a limited way to Chicano literature by the one Chicana professor on the faculty of the English department at the University of Texas at El Paso. I was your basic Anglo-educated, colonized-minded Chicana, militant (but experiential) feminist, and lesbian-in-waiting.

Crossing the sexual border of my identity wasn't like driving over the Córdoba bridge into Juárez. "The awakening of consciousness," says Adrienne Rich, "is not like crossing a frontier—one step and you are in another country."[4] My awakening as a lesbian was more furtive than that. More like wading across the river in the dark, heart pumping as loud as the migra helicopters patrolling the line. More like being caught wet and deported several times. It wasn't until my husband started to censor my writing that I knew I could no longer hide in the safety and privilege, in the fairytale, of a heterosexual marriage. As I said in a poem, "goodbye Peter, hello Rita Mae Brown."[5]

At the time that I was first "experimenting" with woman-love, I was part of a group of Anglo-American dykes. I came out with these women, actually. My first taste of lesbian literature was Desert of the Heart by Jane Rule and Rubyfruit Jungle by Rita

---

[4]See Adrienne Rich, "When We Dead Awaken: Writing as Re-Vision," *Adrienne Rich's Poetry*, ed. Barbara Charlesworth Gelpi and Albert Gelpi, (New York: W.W. Norton, 1975): 90.

[5]From my poem "Leaving 'The Killing Fields,'" *Beggar on the Córdoba Bridge*, a full collection of poems in the volume *Three Times a Woman: Chicana Poetry* (Tempe, AZ: Bilingual Press, 1989): 27. See "Making Tortillas," 44–45. I wrote the "Killing Fields" poem in El Paso in 1983, and the "Tortillera" poem at the end of my Iowa City sojourn in 1986.

Mae Brown; my first lesbian orgasm happened with a white woman; my first *menage-a-trois* was with white women. The first time I realized my life had turned down a different path for good was when I was lying on top of a white woman, and later, another white woman pointed out to me that I loved women too much to ever call myself straight, or even bisexual. In other words, as Harvey Milk would have it, "come out, come out wherever you are." The interesting thing was that when I was around these white women, nobody ever talked about butch/femme; in fact, they frowned on that dyke-otomy, even though everyone looked a lot butchier than I did.

I didn't actually call myself butch. I just knew I was. I knew I liked going to El Noa Noa on Alameda, where the women wore stockings and mascara, and the dykes wore boots and *tejanas*. I liked standing at the bar with my arm around *my* woman. I liked her to watch me shoot pool. I liked feeling her close to me on the dance floor, my right hand pressing at the back of her waist, guiding her to the rhythm of the ballad or the ranchera or the salsa pounding out of the speakers. If any other butch wanted to dance with her, I expected to be asked; she was my woman, after all. I liked ordering her drinks, lighting her cigarette, making her come. I felt like Midas with the golden touch. Any time I brought a woman to orgasm, both of us glowed. I always came after she did, or during, but not before. Ladies first. But when it was my turn, I wanted the same treatment. My breasts, my feet, my armpits, my cunt—everything wanted to be touched, turned to gold.

Now, how, you may ask, did I go from a butch to a tortillera?

I remember it was a Saturday in September, Iowa City, 1985, the day I was invited to my first party of "maricones y tortilleras." I had never heard the term tortillera in a different context than tortilla-maker; all I could see was la señora del mercado sitting by her tin tub of masa clapping tortillas into shape. It took a Cubanidentified Irish-American lesbian to explain to me that tortillera also meant lesbian, not only to the Latino/a gay community of Iowa City in 1985, but to América Latina at large. What's the connection? I asked, between a tortillera and a lesbian? Something to do with the sound, they said, the kneading of masa and palms rubbing together, the clapping of tongues, the intersection of good taste and the golden touch. Thus this Chicana dyke from El Chuco, Texas, was indoctrinated into tortillerismo.[6] I knew that part of the reason that gravity had pulled me to the Midwest had been revealed; I would have to write a poem about this new label, this new identity that smelled of warm, moist corn, that sounded of my Tía Suky's hands patting gorditas in the kitchen. Like lesbian and Chicana, tortillera was originally a derogatory term. But we take it in our mouths, taste the truth of it, and change the meaning. In this way, we begin to own our own names.

I don't know what's worse for my family: that I'm a lesbian or a Chicana. Both terms are equally shameful in their eyes, equally scandalous and worthy of ostracism and oppression. My Chicana self is ridiculed, criticized, invalidated because, according to the people who love me, this is Mexican blood in my veins, and how can I call myself a Chicana if I love la cultura mexicana so much, if I was brought up as a mexicana, if I was never allowed to associate with prietos or Pochos, cholos or pachucos, if I was swatted on the head every time I mixed Spanish with English? When my grandmother received my book of poems, she was very proud, until one of my uncles took it upon himself to act as translator. What a disgrace, what a pity, what a waste of education, they said, that I had the nerve to publish a book and

---

[6]For a review of work done by tortilleras Chicanas since 1981, see my essay, "Tortillerismo: Work by Chicana Lesbians," *Signs: Journal of Women in Culture and Society* 18. 4 (1993): 956–963.

announce, in black print, in English and Spanish words mixed together, that I am "the first Chicana fruit of the family." Needless to say, my grandmother was very upset about my book. That lady who does not know the meaning of political activism, who has never heard of Martin Luther King, Jr. or César Chávez, organized a family boycott so powerful that it nearly catapulted my relationship with the family into oblivion. Again, she refused to talk to me; her silence lasted over a year. My aunt was angry at me for having sent her the book in the first place, but I explained that I had two motivations: I wanted my grandmother to see that what she had called wasting time, the hours I spent hunched over my desk, had produced a body of work worthy of being published, and I didn't want her to say, later, when she found out about the book through somebody else, as she inevitably would, that I hadn't sent her a copy of the book because I was ashamed of my life. To have her or anybody think that I was ashamed of being a lesbian and a Chicana was nothing short of self-betrayal.

Among the many things my grandmother called me, was the epithet *descarada*. In Mexican culture, to have no shame is the equivalent of having no honor, no dignity, no face. To have no face is to be invisible, to be even more devalued than the Mexican peso.

> The world knows us by our faces, the most naked, most vulnerable, exposed and significant topography of the body. When our caras do not live up to the "image" that the family or community wants us to wear and when we rebel against the engraving of our bodies, we experience ostracism, alienation, isolation, and shame.[7]

---

[7] See "Haciendo caras, una entrada/an introduction," *Haciendo Caras/Making Face, Making Soul: Critical and Creative Perspectives by Women of Color*, ed. Gloria Anzaldúa. (San Francisco: aunt lute, 1990): xxiii.

Like Sor Juana Inés de la Cruz, whose story I am telling through my Chicana lesbian/butch/tortillera feminist fronteriza voice and vision,[8] I both resisted the making of my face in my family's/my culture's image, and made my own face, several faces, más caras, through my writing. A través del silencio y de la pluma, me descaré y me hice la cara.

When I stood at the foot of Niagara Falls, another tourist on the Maid of the Mist, the boat was like my consciousness, weighed down by so many contradictions, but at the same time slipping easily through the rainbows that splash out of that relentless cascade; and I realized that, as always, I was in between two countries, and that, like the river, my resistance, my identity, would continue to flow. "The iris is another infinite lesson."

---

[8]See *Sor Juana's Second Dream: A Novel*, (Albuquerque: UNM Press, 1999).

Land of the Dead
(1994–2001)

Carmen's Song

(For my tía, Carmen Gaspar de Alba, 1946–1994)

I.
If God lives, let Her live
in the sausage-shaped tumor
in your bowel,
metastatic shadow
of your womb swimming
in a green liquid
ovaries like swollen secrets
from which it has taken you
47 years and 2 surgeries
to emerge.

Today the border has compressed
into those thin lines of the CT scan,
"risk of anesthesia death"
scrawled carelessly on your chart.
Your patience astounds me,
the daily courage
you scrape like gold
or ashes
from the rocky bottom
of your heart.

We bring you mariachis
for your birthday
on the front lawn.
The neighbors gather
to witness another Mexican

fiesta. This is El Paso.
You don't let the morphine
catheter bother you
while you dance.

II.
The plane flies over the Rockies.
I remember watching you die once
when I was five years old.
Talking on the phone
you crumpled to the floor.
I bolted down the street
screaming *"mi tía se murió."*
A neighbor walked me home.
Your brothers, like guardian angels,
had brought you back to life.
You were sitting up in bed, faint
with grief, your best friend
had been killed in a car accident.

Honey, you were my first proof
of resurrection.

Turbulence over the desert.
I have rubbed your feet for the last time.
Nine days from now you will choose
to die on December 12th,
Día de la Virgen de Guadalupe,
day of your mother's birth.

III.
The lilac coffin
borne by five mujeres fuertes
(all of us one kind
of Honey or another)
is a clue. Nobody knows
how you managed
to choreograph the fluid
figure 8's of the police bikes
escorting our caravan
to the cemetery.
The burnt smell in the air
is not wood smoke but silence.

IV.
Duquesa, you will not sleep
next to your father or two brothers,
no more room in the family plot,
but here, under junipers and desert light,
the weight of the Guadalupe peaks
crushing rib and cranium.
Your pelvis hollowed now
after the surgeries
and the hunger of five months—
a niche for your mother's love
to glow, candles
rather than nightlights
to guide her through the dark.

V.
Flaca, I can still see you dancing,
cumbia, ranchera, rock and roll.
"Está loca," my grandmother would say,
watching you dust the furniture and spin
in the air to an Elvis Presley tune,
sing into the broom handle con las Supremes.

You loved to dance with other women.
You're the one
who taught me how to lead,
classy movidas on the dance floor.

Trust your feet, you said, hold her close
enough so she knows exactly
where you want to go, but always
con respeto, your hand
light as a white glove.

Use your father's charm, you said,
your tía's knowledge
of what a woman wants.
A lady loves a confident dancer.

Blackjack

"The heart weighs 300 gms."

—Coroner's Report

My father died on a redwood swing
banking the Ruidoso River.
Lucky to the last day of his broken-
hearted life. I can think of worse ways to go.
The way his brother's brain
must have imploded from that bullet
to the head. Or how his youngest brother
got ejected from a speeding car, spine
like kindling fifty feet from the accident.
Or the way the large omental cake,
the tumorous plaque, the carboplatin
pumping through the port-o-cath
ate away at his sister's entrails.

Last summer my little brother's naked body
was found under a bridge, flesh so decomposed
even his fingerprints had been gnawed away.
My mother's name (my name) —Teyali—
tattooed on his right arm.
Short life summarized in lockdown lettering
and the invisible ink of his addiction.
Plastic bag over his face, he died
with his tongue clenched tight between his teeth.
Now a bronze Guadalupe guards his ashes
in front of the Zaragosa Bridge.

The bridge between the living and the dead
was the swing where my father smoked his last cigarette
that morning in the cool mountain piñón breeze,
his mother serving breakfast on the deck
and the river splashing over smooth rocks. Thud
of skull against wood and his cigarette still burning
in the ashtray. Embolism ended his winning streak
at the Inn of the Mountain Gods forever.

Didn't go to his funeral, but today, eleven years later,
I stand beside that swing, take
a picture of it, and the men with young sons
fishing from the other bank
reel his guilt out of the river:
three aces dealt to him like children
and no insurance to hedge his bets. Sudden death
his ultimate blackjack.

Culto a la Muerte: Oaxaca, 1999

It is one week before the dead
are brought to life in the cemetery
celebrations of Día de los Muertos.
Children squeal through the mercado,
treasure hunt for calaveras with their names
encrusted on the sugary skulls.

You walk across town carrying two tall bundles
of gladiolas—red and white—the colors of Changó,
una promesa you made
ten years ago to la Virgen de la Soledad.

At the mezcal distillery
you could lose your head
or your lunch just on the fumes.
The smell of agave juice squeezed hot
from the blue hearts of cactus
cooked in a pit of mesquite
coals for three days.

The stone pressing the spirit
out of the soft yellow flesh
could be a calendar stone
or a medieval torture wheel
pulled round and round by a burro
drunk on the essence of maguey
fermenting in the wooden vats.

There are two altars here.
On a repisa next to the door, our Lady of Refugio,
gilt-framed between thick white candles,
yellow *cempasúchil* and dried beans.
Across the room, a clay goddess
locked in an iron niche,
radiant halo of corn
cobs and agave spears:
she speaks Zapotec, says our guide.
Serpents and jaguars on the walls.
All guardians of the cycle—vida y muerte.

Sabor del dolor distilled
into a fine gold liquid laced with wood smoke
and a native worm
to remind you where you're going.
Keep the faith.

Witch Museum

"Long after Christianity had come, witchcraft survived in secret. On the Witch's Sabbath, the covens of thirteen would gather around their magic nine-foot circle, the fire would be lit beneath the cauldron, the scourge and pentacle and atham—the black-handled sacrificial knife—would appear and the ancient ritual invoking the evil one would begin."
                                    —postcard of the Sabbat Circle
                                        at the Salem Witch Museum

I.
Fork up $2.75
and gather 'round
this scarlet Sabbath circle
inscribed with names all
witches worship, as you know.

> Ashtaroth
> Astarte   Baphomet
> Beelzebub   Asmodeus
> Lucifer Rex

If you're innocent
or just curious as a cat
with lives to spare,
take your coat off,
have a seat (but don't
let foot or finger touch
the magic symbols if you know
what's good for you).

Twenty
minutes of the past
won't kill you.

Watch the story return to life
in thirteen
Techno Sight and Sound
individually fired-up
scenes, latest concept
in witch museums.

II.
In France, a whirl of autumn
leaves makes girls
cry out *"les sorcieres!"*

In a northern province
of Argentina, old women
step out of their houses
and talk to the wind:
"ya van cuatro tardes de viento,"
they say, and the wind
whistles their names
through the holes
of the cardos, petrified
sentinels of cactus
that line the crooked streets
of their solitude.

Where I come from
the wind is more alive
than the people's memory,
the border
between life and death
is called the Rio Bravo
and sand spinning
in the desert
a sure sign
of dust devils
come to drag you
out of your bed at night,
come to feast
on the bones of the girls
in blue smocks,
three hundred dead women
and counting.

No gift shops,
no souvenir Norwegian witches
or scarlet circles to manifest
the presence of those
who have never left.
Wind and leaf and sand are enough
if all we need is to be reminded.

Kyrie Eleison for La Llorona

I.
I'm not saying she died.

I'm not saying she no longer lives
in the weeping willows of Iowa City,
the Boston Common, or el Chamizal.

I'm not saying she is no longer
seen on the Zaragosa bridge,
the Golden Gate, or the Longfellow.

Nor that her cries have ceased
pulling stray kids and lovers
to her path, her veiled bed

always vacant on one side.
It's just that, for all her years
in our genealogy, all the blame

she's always borne for everybody's sins,
nobody's ever offered a mass
for La Llorona, wicked mother

grieving on the riverbank,
wailing through the streets,
haunting the causeways

of our island-hearts.
Nobody's ever asked
why she is still

not canonized, devil's martyr.

II.
You find four

chrysanthemums on the sidewalk,
four yellow heads
without stems or leaves,

without roots or veins.
One smells of hospital, of liniment
and alcohol, of an old man's gums.

Another has the odor of a dance,
quinceañera dress streaked
with semen and blood.

The third one has the look of a secret.
Aroma of sea salt, fish bones,
lunar cave and cobwebs.

And this one, last handful of light,
mums its truth between the petals,
a tart yellow essence

that could be dog urine
or the seed of the forbidden fruit
or the heart that sows

the cornfield of the sun.

III.
Llorona, yours is the satisfaction of having been

every conquistador's idea
of a wet dream,
every child's fear of drowning.

Patron saint of bus stops and turnstiles.
Virgin of the deported.
Mother of the dispossessed.

You've gone the way of the alligators
in San Jacinto Plaza.
You've traded your midnight cry for the graveyard

shift and a paycheck at the maquila.
That mushroom cloud hovering
over mount Cristo Rey

is your shadow.
That train howling past the gay bars of El Paso
is what's left of your voice.

The smell of these chrysanthemums
burning is the incense
of your memory.

Lord, have mercy.

Eclipse (September 11th): New York City, 2001

If you look closely September Eleventh
is an abstract way of saying goodbye
another square on the calendar
another day's agenda to beam
from the handheld to the cell phone:
pack a bag, take a shower, call a taxi.

On the elevator to the 78th floor
a secretary burns her tongue on hot coffee.
Office is closed today but there's an urgent
fax she forgot to send last night.
Her boss sits down to bagels
and a view of the early autumn skyline
from his Battery Park apartment.

At Logan airport someone
is admiring his new shoes,
someone washes her hands in the bathroom,
someone pins a nametag on a child, promises
Disneyland next summer.

In a frighteningly common act, they board
the planes that will propel
them to a collective blazing destiny
inside the World Trade Center, zero
degrees of separation
as they melt
into each other's bones.

The square on the calendar is black
now from the smoke, the bodies
that never learned to fly
to choose the flames or the street
one hundred floors below.

There were some who knew the square
was more than an abstraction,
who knew the ending of the story
meant the last day of their lives
who felt a tinge of sadness
on their tongue like bitter tea
gulped down before take-off
a rush of devotion pure
as adrenaline or caffeine.

Human sacrifice as old as Huitzilopochtli
now Bin Laden, Bush, Yahweh, Mohammed—
all war gods
feeding on the hearts
of the chosen.

Can you see her?
There at Ground Zero:
that is not Liberty
walking among the dead,
wearing a hard hat
and a gas mask
black hair dragging in the ashes
of all those nameless Mexicans.
That woman wailing at the sooty sky
is La Llorona.

She knows the towers
will topple like Babel,
like the tarot card
that signifies the end
of an old world order.

In Cedar Falls, Iowa, September Eleventh
is my friend Sara's birthday
forever marked now with the abstract
logic of sacrifice,
twin lightning bolts
of revenge
or redemption.

El Encuentro

Butch played with the cold calamari. Now there was a trail of pale fried squid rings between the white plate and the empty shot glasses and the snifters. A chain of small open mouths tinged with tomato sauce on the black bar. Walt, the barman, blond as a beach boy and big on contradictions, snapped a wet towel over his shoulder.

"Hey, Butch, how 'bout letting me clean up some of this mess?"

"And have me lose count of how much I hate myself?"

"Sorry, Butch, it's getting busy and I'm running out of glasses."

Walt wiped the calamaris off the bar with the towel, gathered the glasses in two clumps and ran them under the soapy water in the sink.

On Saturdays from six to seven-forty-five the bar was packed with Schubert Theater types sipping Bellinis and flutes of bubbly before the show, but now it was a younger crowd, mostly couples, mostly from Westwood, waiting for their tables to open in the dining room. Not the kind of bar patrons you could sit beside and exchange life's-a-beach-and-then-you-die comments with or even eavesdrop on a rant about the latest traffic jam on the 405. It was Valentine's Day and all they wanted to do was make out in public.

Butch had invited the new assistant professor in her department for a drink at five in the afternoon to beat the theater rush, but it was now nearly nine and Butch had to accept she wasn't coming. She was either married or too politically correct to go out with a lesbian colleague whose nickname was Butch.

Butch ordered another Scotch. Earlier it was Cuervo in double shots to warm up from the wet walk down Avenue of the Stars under a ripped umbrella. After a couple of hours of craning her neck each time the door opened and catching a draft of El Niño like a slap in the face, Butch had moved on to gin martinis, straight-up, extra cold. But the taste of the olive reminded her too much of the woman she was not sleeping with anymore, whose name she would not allow herself to think, and so she had changed to single malt whiskey in a snifter. Walt tipped the Glenlivet bottle over her glass and poured Butch another healthy shot. Butch took a hit of the Glenlivet, smoky peat in her nostrils.

On the stool next to hers the guy chugging Millers from the bottle turned and leered at her again. He and she and Walt were the only singles in the place. Butch could tell he was getting ready to make his move.

"Hey, Walt!" she called out. "I need a girlfriend. My date didn't show."

The Millers guy burped in her face and turned his back on her. The air stunk of beer and antipasto.

"Thought you were finished with women," said Walt, mixing up yet another corny Valentine's drink with strawberries.

"Just ones like the one in P. V." Butch could tell she was slurring her abbreviations.

She had gone to Puerto Vallarta to get inspired for a new play. Found a room with a terrace overlooking the River Cuale for seven bucks, and a nearby piano dive rumored to be a gay bar. She had not met anyone until the last night, one of the local girls sitting alone at the little table by the door who kept drinking the margaritas that Butch told the bartender to put on her tab. After the third one, Butch thought it was time for introductions.

"Vanessa." The girl said her name in a smoky whisper. The girl's hands were rough, her fingers thick and calloused, like a maid's.

"Pleasure," said Butch, pulling her chair close enough to

smell the gardenias in the girl's perfume. The girl's front teeth were edged in gold, and gold lights streaked her loose brown hair. They talked and smoked and drank and Butch was happy except when the bartender or the waiter or the doorman came over and stood behind them acting like they needed to say something to Butch. Finally Butch asked the girl to dance and told the guys to stop hovering over their table. The girl writhed her thin body on the crowded dance floor and clung to Butch's arm when they left the bar and walked along the *malecón* listening to the surf slap against the rocks on the beach.

The night clerk of the Hotel Saavedra was watching his television behind the desk and did not see them kissing in the shadows of the foyer. Butch had the girl pushed up against the wall, palming her pubescent breasts over her polyester blouse.

"Let's go to my room," Butch said, but the girl refused to go upstairs with her.

"Are you afraid or ashamed?" Butch asked.

The girl shook her head and started to cry. "It's just that I'm not what you think," she said. "That's what those guys in the bar were trying to tell you."

"What are you talking about?" said Butch, slipping her hand between the girl's legs.

"Don't," said the girl, "please don't touch my neutral part."

She wiped her nose on Butch's collar and asked for cab fare. Butch walked her to the taxi stand on the next block. The next day she found out from the doorman of the bar that Vanessa's real name was Bruno.

"Earth to Butch," said Walt.

The Millers guy was gone and Walt was placing a house drink—Campari and gin in a martini glass—in front of the woman who was now sitting beside Butch.

"I assume this seat isn't taken," she said.

114

Butch shook her head and swallowed hard.

The woman raised her translucent red drink for a toast. "Happy Valentine's Day," she said. Butch was polite. She toasted.

The woman's lipstick left an impression on the edge of the glass. Butch remembered the open mouths of the calamari. Her belly turned to squid.

"Do I know you?" Butch asked.

"You must," said the woman, "you've been on my track for years."

Acknowledgments

The following pieces have been previously published, some in slightly different versions.

"Literary Wetback," *The Massachusetts Review* XXIX.2 (1988): 242–246. Reprinted in *Infinite Divisions: An Anthology of Chicana Literature*, eds. Tey Diana Rebolledo and Eliana Rivero (Tempe, AZ: University of Arizona Press, 1993): 288–292.

"Crooked Foot Speaks/Habla Pata Chueca," "After 21 Years, A Postcard from My Father," "In the Shadow of Greater Things," "Bamba Basílica," "Dust to Dust," and "Holy Ground," *The Americas Review* 16.3–4 (1988): 49–56.

"Caldo de Pollo" and "Sor Juana's Litany in the Subjunctive" (under a different title), *The Blue Mesa Review* 2 (1990): 81–83.

"Karmic Revolution," *The Boston Review* (1990): 3.

"Pilgrim's Progress," *The Taos Review* 3 (1990): 166–167.

"The Philosophy of Frijoles," *Hanging Loose* 57 (1990): 26.

"Gardenias for El Gran Gurú," "I Dream of Galloping," and "Autumn Equinox in the Sandias," *Puerto Del Sol: Special Caló Issue* (1992): 94–100.

"Elemental Journey," *After Aztlán: Latino Poets in the Nineties* (Boston: David Godine Publishers, 1992): 64–74.

"Descarada/No Shame," *The Wild Good: Lesbian Photographs and Writings about Love*, ed. Beatrix Gates (New York: Anchor Books, 1996): 217–223. Reprinted in *The Rio Grande Review* 19.1 (Spring 2000): 150–159.

"After 21 Years a Postcard from My Father" and "Bamba Basílica," reprinted in *The Floating Borderlands. Twenty-Five Years Of U.S. Hispanic Literature*, ed. Lauro Flores (Seattle: University of Washington Press, 1998): 235–238.

"Sor Juana's Litany in the Subjunctive" and "The Waters of Grief," *The Americas Review* 25: 1–2 (1999): 93–96. "Sor Juana's Litany in the Subjunctive" was also reprinted in my novel, *Sor Juana's Second Dream* (Albuquerque: University of New Mexico Press, 1999): 457.

"Blackjack" and "Neighbors," *Colorado Review* XXVII (Summer 2000): 18–21.

"Kyrie Eleison for La Llorona," *Tongues Magazine* vol 1 (2001): 5–6.

"Chamizal" and "Witch Museum" in *This Bridge We Call Home: Radical Visions for Transformation*, eds. Gloria Anzaldúa and Analouise Keating (New York: Routledge, 2002): 483–485, 517–519.

"Listening to Our Bones" won second place in the 2002 Ann Stanford Poetry Prize sponsored by the Writing Program at the University of Southern California. It will be published in *Southern California Anthology* 19 (Summer 2003).